Children Also Grieve

of related interest

Someone Very Important Has Just Died
Immediate Help for People Caring for Children of All Ages
at the Time of a Close Bereavement
Mary Turner
ISBN 1 84310 295 1

Talking with Children and Young People about Death and Dying
A Workbook
Mary Turner
ISBN 1 85302 563 1

A Safe Place for Caleb
An Interactive Book for Kids, Teens, and Adults with Issues of Attachment,
Grief and Loss, or Early Trauma
Kathleen A. Chara and Paul J. Chara, Jr.
ISBN 1 84310 799 6

Helping Children to Manage Loss
Positive Strategies for Renewal and Growth
Brenda Mallon
ISBN 1 85302 605 0

Without You – Children and Young People Growing Up with Loss and its Effects
Tamar Granot
ISBN 1 84310 297 8

The Forgotten Mourners, Second Edition
Guidelines for Working with Bereaved Children
Susan C. Smith
ISBN 1 85302 758 8

Grief in Children
A Handbook for Adults
Atle Dyregrov
ISBN 1 85302 113 X

Children Also Grieve
Talking about Death and Healing

Linda Goldman

Photographs by Linda Goldman

Jessica Kingsley Publishers
London and Philadelphia

Photograph of Ling on p.10 reproduced with kind permission from Mike Lee.

First published in 2006
by Jessica Kingsley Publishers
116 Pentonville Road
London N1 9JB, UK
and
400 Market Street, Suite 400
Philadelphia, PA 19106, USA

www.jkp.com

Library of Congress Cataloging in Publication Data
Goldman, Linda, 1946-
  Children also grieve : talking about death and healing / Linda Goldman.-- 1st American hardcover ed.
    p. cm.
  Includes bibliographical references.
  ISBN-13: 978-1-84310-808-5 (hardcover : alk. paper)
  ISBN-10: 1-84310-808-9 (hardcover : alk. paper) 1. Grief in children. 2. Bereavement in children. 3. Children and death. I. Title.
  BF723.G75G642 2005
  155.9'37'083--dc22
                         2005014317

British Library Cataloguing in Publication Data
A CIP catalogue record for this book is available from the British Library

ISBN-13: 978 1 84310 808 5
ISBN-10: 1 84310 808 9

Printed and bound in the People's Republic of China APC-FT3929

A strong tree grows from a carefully tended sapling.
The education of people begins with youth.

— Popular proverb

Contents

Henry's Story

Hi. My name is **Henry**.

Grandfather has died and I am very sad. I live with my friends Ling, Suzie, and Yili. Tashi and Sam live nearby.

This is the story of our grief and the ways we have learned to heal.

This is **Ling**. He is five years old. He is the little brother of Suzie and Yili. He has been sad since Grandfather died and doesn't feel like playing ball anymore.

This is **Suzie**. She is Ling and Yili's sister. She is fifteen years old. Even though Grandfather died, she is still happy and likes to sing and dance.

This is **Yili**. He is the older brother of Ling and Suzie. He is sixteen years old. He is angry that Grandfather died.

This is my friend **Tashi**. She lives next door to me and visits a lot. I can talk to her about my feelings about Grandfather and she will listen.

This is **Sam**. He lives across the street in a big brown house. Tashi and I used to chase Sam. When Grandfather died it didn't seem like fun anymore.

Ling, Suzie, and Yili are grieving the death of their grandfather. Grandfather lived at home with them and their mom, dad, and me until he died. Tashi and Sam miss him too. We all miss Grandfather very much.

Sometimes it's hard to talk about death. But death is a part of life. It is a natural part of life. We are born, we live, we grow old, we die. This is natural.

Life has many changes, just like the seasons. Animals, plants, and people die. New animals, plants, and people are born, and life continues.

Grandfather died in winter. It felt cold and lonely.

I tried to play in the snow with my friend Tashi so that I would forget about how bad I felt. But I still felt bad. Playing with Tashi didn't seem like fun anymore. Nothing did.

Winter felt long and I felt empty inside. I didn't want to dig, or chase Sam the cat, or even bury a bone. My heart hurt.

I thought the sun would never shine again.

Then springtime came.
I began to feel better. Yili
told me it was ok to feel
better. I could still love
Grandfather and miss
him, but I could start to
be happy again too.

We began taking walks
by the lake. It was so
pretty.

We decided to plant pink spring flowers for
Grandfather. Pink was his favorite color.

14

Can you tell me what you think death is?

I think death is when the body stops
working. Usually people die when they are
very, very old, or very, very sick, or so
injured that the doctors and nurses can't
keep their bodies working.

When someone dies…

   …they can't eat candy

   …they can't watch TV

   …they can't sing

   …they can't play

   …they can't breathe.

Their body doesn't work anymore.

Ling wanted to know how Grandfather died. Mother said he was very, very old, and got very, very sick. He went to the hospital because he was feeling very sick. His heart stopped working, and he died.

People can die in many ways…

They can get hit by a car or crash in a plane.   They can die from a serious illness.

They can die of old age.

They can decide to make their body stop working and kill themselves. This is called suicide.

They can fall off the roof or drown swimming.

Someone else can kill them.
This is called murder.

They can be soldiers and get killed in war.

How did the person you knew die?

Sometimes grief can hit us like waves from the ocean.

When someone dies, we grieve. Grief can be feelings of sadness, anger, worry, fear, and loneliness. Many people have these feelings after the death of a person they care about.

Sometimes grief hits me like waves from the ocean. I never know when a wave of grief will hit me or how it will make me feel. A bird flying, a song on the radio, or a beautiful butterfly can suddenly remind me that Grandfather is not here anymore. I might burst into tears or bark at a friend.

Often I feel like hiding my feelings because it seems no one understands, or I'm worried that people might make fun of me. I don't like to feel different.

Are there any feelings you hide? Tell me what they are.

I am worried about my friends Ling, Suzie, and Yili. Ling used to play ball with me, and we would all go for long walks in the park. Now Ling feels too sad because Grandfather has died.

Have you ever felt too sad to play? What made you feel so sad?

Once I felt angry at Grandfather for dying. Then I felt ashamed for feeling like that towards Grandfather.

Have you ever felt ashamed about a feeling you've had towards the person who died? Tell me about it.

Sometimes we get angry when someone dies, and feel like yelling or screaming or even hitting someone. Angry feelings are ok.

Yili is my big friend. He is sad and angry too. Yili yelled at me for lying on his bed with muddy paws. He had never done that before. He said he was sorry and wanted to think of some ways to let out his anger without hurting himself or someone else.

What makes you angry?

Here are some things you could do when you are angry…

Tell someone why you are angry.

Go outside and run like the wind.

Write an angry letter about how you feel.
You don't need to send it.

Yell in the shower.

Play football.

Talk to a friend.

Punch a ball or pillow.

What can you do when you feel angry?

Suzie is Ling and Yili's sister. Since Grandfather died, Suzie still acts happy. She laughs, sings, dances, and says she feels fine.

Everyone grieves in different ways. This is ok.

There are days when I feel like I'm in a cage with no way to get out. I feel trapped with all of my feelings and thoughts.

Do you ever feel trapped with your feelings and thoughts, and don't know how to let them out? Tell me about them. It may help you to feel better.

Everyone gets scared at times. Suzie told me she got frightened that her mom and dad would die too, and didn't know who would take care of her. This scares lots of kids.

Is there something that scares you? Tell me about it. Sharing something that scares you can take some of the fear away.

Feelings can live in our bodies and hurt like aches and pains. We might get headaches or stomach aches, or we could even feel dizzy. Some people can't eat or sleep.

Where in your body do you feel your feelings? Tell me about them.

Sometimes I think it was my fault Grandfather died. If only I had taken better care of him, given him more medicine, or not let him go out in the cold. One time I got angry and growled at Grandfather for moving so slowly, and maybe that made him even sicker.

Do you have any "If onlys"? – things you worry may have caused the person you knew to die. What are they?

It is important to know that people can't die because of what we think, say, or wish. Death is not like magic. Our thoughts and feelings don't make people die.

GRRRRRRR

Sometimes I think about the friends I can talk to when I'm feeling sad, or angry, or scared, or lonely. I remember that Tashi is my best friend, and I feel better when I share my feelings with her.

We can share grief with…

…teachers

…moms and dads

…aunts and uncles

…babysitters

…cousins

…sisters and brothers

…friends and neighbors

…God, a spirit, or nature

…and even pets.

Who can you share your grief with?

How do you share your grief?

How does it make you feel to share your grief?

Sometimes it feels good just to ask
for a hug.

Often I wonder where Grandfather is. I look at the sky and I can almost see his face in the clouds or hear his voice in the wind.

What do you wonder about?

Have you ever felt that the person you knew who has died was with you in some way? Maybe a breeze that blew against your cheek or a beautiful butterfly that rested on a flower. What was that like? Tell me about it.

When the doorbell rings, sometimes Tashi and I wonder if it is Grandfather at the door. Although we know it can't be him, we still wonder.

Ling told me he had a dream about Grandfather. He said Grandfather was running with me in a big field, and then he lay down with me in the grass and looked at all of the beautiful flowers. It made me feel good to hear Ling's dream about Grandfather.

Have you ever had a dream about your special person? Tell me about it.

Ling, Suzie, Yili, and I had many questions after Grandfather died…

Will I die, or will anyone else that I know?   Why do I feel so bad?

Why did Grandfather die?

What happens after someone dies?

Did Grandfather suffer?

Is it ok to talk about Grandfather?

Is it my fault Grandfather died?

What questions do you have about the person who died?

"Where is Grandfather?" is one question I have.

Some people say Grandfather is in heaven, others say he is with God. One of my friends told me Grandfather might come back again in another form – maybe as a plant or animal, or as another person. Tashi said Grandfather is buried in the ground and he helps the plants and animals to grow.

Grandfather would say life and death are mysteries. There may be more to understanding the world than we can possibly imagine.

Where do you think the person you knew is now?

Life is different after someone dies. Tashi and I played tag and chased the neighbor's goose before Grandfather died.

After he died I felt tired a lot and just wanted to rest.

I needed to be alone in a quiet and peaceful place. I would often sit in Grandfather's chair when I missed him. It helped me.

When Yili missed him, he visited Grandfather's grave. Suzie wrote poetry. Ling sat with me. Sam took naps on Grandfather's bed. Tashi listened to music that reminds her of Grandfather.

Sometimes I would sit by the water, feel the breeze on my face, and watch the fish swim by.

Other times I felt safe and protected inside a shelter by the lake. I listened to the birds chirping, and it reminded me of Grandfather singing to me.

Where do you go to feel safe and peaceful?

Tell me about your peaceful place.

Tashi came over to take me to a friend's birthday party. I decided not to go. I didn't want to be around anyone. She said that was ok.

This made me feel better.

The next week Tashi came back and asked if we could play. This time I said yes.

Tashi said it was ok to miss Grandfather and still have fun.

We played hide and seek. I stayed very still behind the bushes.

We pretended to be statues. That was a fun game.

It felt good to laugh again. Grandfather would have laughed too. He loved to watch us play.

What do you do to have fun?

Sometimes we just sat and talked about Grandfather.

A friend is someone who listens and understands. Tashi is my friend and I know I can trust her. She helps me by letting me share a memory or just by sitting with me without saying anything.

Who are your friends?

Tell me about a time you shared a memory with a friend.

After Grandfather died, I shared memories with my family too.
I learned so much about Grandfather, and it felt good to
talk about him.

Ling said Grandfather loved to fly kites with him.

Suzie said Grandfather told her wonderful stories at bedtime.

Yili said Grandfather taught him to fish.

I said Grandfather gave me treats.

We can share memories in many ways.

We can make a **memory book**.

A memory book is a special place to write or draw memories about a person who has died. The second half of this book is blank for you to fill in and use as your own memory book, but if you want to make your own you can write in a blank scrapbook or ask your mom or dad to help you make one.

We can make a **memory table** of special items that remind us of the person who has died. Just lay a tablecloth over a table and place your special objects on the cloth. You might like to take a photograph of them.

Ling put Grandfather's hat on the table.

Suzie added Grandfather's pipe.

Yili brought out Grandfather's clock.

We put Grandfather's favorite roses in a vase.

We can also make a **memory mural**, **collage**, or **video**.

We can make a **memory photo album** of our life together. We can write a story about it. Collect as many photos as you can of the person who has died. Put these into an album or a scrapbook. You can write messages to remind you when the pictures were taken and what they mean to you.

We can make a **memory box** and decorate it with pictures and things that remind us of the person who has died. You could paint an old shoe box or a cardboard box and decorate it with stickers or drawings. Then put something special inside that reminds you of your special person. Yili put in Grandfather's watch.

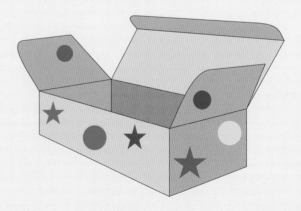

Yili, Suzie, and Ling did some things to remember Grandfather…

They went to his funeral.

They drew a picture.

They planted flowers.

They lit a candle.

They wrote a poem.

They sang Grandfather's favorite song.

They sent off a balloon.

I like to remember Grandfather. I use rituals to remember. Rituals are things I can do to help me remember Grandfather in nice ways. Here are a few favorites.

Some of my friends like to say a prayer, draw a heart, write a story, or look at a photograph. I like to make paw prints in the snow.

What rituals do you use to remember your person? Tell me about them.

Special birthdays and holidays can remind us of the person we knew who has died. We can use rituals to remember them on these days. Yili, Tashi, and I decided to fly a kite with an "I Love You" note attached on Grandfather's birthday. The sky was glowing that morning.

What are your family rituals for special days?

Did you get to say goodbye to the person you knew who died?

Tashi and I went to Grandfather's funeral. We got to say goodbye, tell him we love him, and thank him for loving us so much.

Now I know I can talk about Grandfather and share my memories of him. It helps me to feel better when I miss him.

Grandfather will always be a part of me. He lives in my heart.

This part of the book is for you to fill in about your special person.

My Memory Book

My name is ……………………………I am …… years old.

This is a picture of me:

My special person is ……………………………

Here is a picture of my special person:

………………………… was born on ……………………………

and died on ……………………………

.... told me that ....

had died.

.... died because:

This is how .... died:

Memory projects can help us to remember a person.

We can make a memory table.

This is what I would put on my memory table:

We can make a memory box.

This is what I would put inside my memory box:

We can make a memory photo album.

Here are some pictures of my life:

My favorite memory is:

My funniest memory is:

If I could have one wish it would be:

If I could say one more thing to ………………………… it would be:

Sometimes I feel like writing a letter to ....

Here's what I would say:

Dear ....

Love from

....

Here is a picture of my family:

Their names are ....

....

....

This is how each person in my family grieves:

This is a picture of my family before .... died:

This is a picture of my family after .... died:

Here is a picture of the friends I can talk to about my grief:

These are their names and telephone numbers:

Name   Telephone number

. . . .

. . . .

. . . .

. . . .

Here is a picture of my favorite pet:

This pet's name is ……………………………

This is the way my pet helps me grieve:

Here are some feelings kids have when they are grieving. Circle the ones you have felt since …………………………… died.

Sad	Worried	Sorry	Guilty
Lonely	Happy	Revengeful	Hopeful
Unprotected	Scared	Shocked	Surprised
Angry	Ashamed	Wondering	Nervous

I have lots of feelings.

Right now I am feeling………………………………………because:

This is how I would draw or write about the following feelings:

Sad

Angry

Scared

Happy

Guilty

Confused

This is something I worry about:

Here are my five main worries:

1..

2..

3..

4..

5..

One thing I am sorry about is:

One thing I am hoping for is:

Circle something you want to do for your person:

Plant a flower   Send off a balloon   Write a poem

Or do something special such as:

These are the things I really liked about .... :

This is something I learned from .... :

I went to the funeral. This is what it was like:

If I could say goodbye now, I would say:

.... will always be in my heart.

Sharing Grief with Words

Casket or **coffin** is a box that a dead person's body is placed in. It is then buried in the ground.

Cemetery is a place where caskets and coffins are buried. Many people are buried there. Pets can be buried there too.

Death is when a person's body stops working.

Depression is a feeling of hopelessness and sadness that doesn't seem to go away.

Faith is the belief that life will be ok again.

Friends are people who listen and care. You can trust them and know they will be there for you if you need them. Animals can be friends too.

Funeral is a gathering of friends and family where children and adults come together to remember the person who has died and say goodbye.

Grave is a place at the cemetery where the casket with the dead body is placed. It is marked with a name so friends and relatives can visit it.

Grief is a feeling of sadness, anger, worry, fear, or loneliness after someone dies.

Guilt is a feeling that it is our fault that something has happened.

Homicide or **murder** is when someone makes someone else's body stop working.

Memory is remembering something that happened in the past.

Revenge is a deep feeling of wanting to hurt someone because you think they hurt you.

Rituals are behaviors we can use to express grief, for example, lighting a candle.

Shame is feeling guilty about something we have done that we don't want anyone to know about.

Suicide is when someone makes his or her own body stop working.

Trauma is something unexpected that happens that might feel scary and bad.

We are *powerless* to control the losses and catastrophic events our children may need to face. But by honoring their inner wisdom, providing mentorship, and creating safe havens for expression, we can *empower* them to become more capable and more caring human beings.

Linda Goldman
Raising Our Children to Be Resilient *(2005)*

For Caring Adults

Sometimes it is difficult for parents, educators, and other caring professionals to talk to children about grief and loss. Often adults may consciously or unconsciously inhibit children from expressing feelings due to their own discomfort or inability to speak of death. For many girls and boys it may be easier to talk with a fictional character or imaginary friend about their private emotions.

Children Also Grieve opens the discussion of grief-related issues with vocabulary that children can understand. The storyline is simple and characters are familiar to children, and Henry explains his thoughts and feelings about the death of Grandfather in child-friendly terms.

Henry defines death for children as "when the body stops working" and speaks of the sadness, anger, fear, and loneliness the loss of a loved one can bring. He also speaks of healing and the ability to enjoy life and still love Grandfather. Henry knows he can carry Grandfather in his heart.

Common signs of grief

Adults and children need to gain an awareness of the common signs of grief in order to feel reassurance, reduce anxiety, and normalize the experience of death. Educators, counselors, clergy, parents, and other caring professionals can identify these signs as a "cry for help". Girls and boys learn that they share common forms of expressing thoughts and feelings and that these thoughts and feelings are often similar to those of other bereaved children. The following are common grief responses.

Grieving children:

- tell and retell their story

- are preoccupied with death, their own health, and the health of their friends and family

- speak of the person who has died in the present tense

- feel the presence of the deceased loved one

- tend to imitate and idolize their loved one who has died

- become the class clown, class bully, or withdraw from others

- show an inability to concentrate, and appear to daydream

- experience nightmares, bedwetting, or regress and become clingy

- complain of stomach aches and headaches

- yearn to be with the deceased loved one.

Children's view of death

The Swiss educator Piaget explained that young children – sually between the ages of two and seven – are categorized as part of the pre-operational stage of cognitive development. During this stage, girls and boys exhibit magical thinking, egocentricity, reversibility, and causality in the way they view death.

Children think their words and thoughts can *magically* cause a person to die. Adam screamed at his older brother, "I hate you and I wish you were dead!" He was then haunted by the idea that this wish created his brother's fatal car accident. Adam's *egocentric* perception meant that he saw himself at the center of the universe, capable of creating and destroying at will the world around him. He blamed himself, saying over and over again that he knew his "words made his brother die." This is an example of a common reaction to bereavement in young children: they feel that they have been the *cause* of a loved one's death.

Mira, a six-year-old whose dad also died in an car accident, visualized death as *reversible* and thought her dad was going to come back. She wrote a letter to her dad and sent it in the mail to heaven. She waited and waited for a letter back, even though she knew her dad was killed in the crash.

Children between the ages of seven and twelve are generally a part of the concrete operational stage of cognitive development. This means that they want to know facts about how their person died. They have a more realistic concept of time, and are beginning to develop their spiritual belief system.

Jimmy is an eight-year-old whose magical thinking convinced him that he had killed his mother. He explained that his mother picked him up the night she had her heart attack – he was four. "If she hadn't done that, she wouldn't have died. It's all my fault," he said. In this stage of their development, children want to know more about the person who has died. Explaining the *medical facts* to Jimmy was very helpful. He learned what caused his mother's heart attack. Being overweight, not taking medication, and smoking cigarettes were important factors. Using age-appropriate facts as a reality check had a comforting effect on Jimmy.

Clichés that inhibit the grief process

Children often take language literally. They need direct and simple language explaining death. When defining death for the young child we could say, "Death is when the body stops working. Usually someone dies when they are very, very old, or very, very sick, or their bodies are so injured that the doctors and nurses can't make their bodies work again." The following are examples of children's reactions to common clichés that can hinder the grief process.

Grandmother told Jen, "Grandfather went on a long trip." Jen questioned this: "Why didn't he say goodbye and why didn't he take me with him?" She waited for him to come back.

Lin heard in nursery school that her friend, Sumi, lost her mother. "How could she lose her?" she asked in a panicked voice. "She was so big."

"Do you think Dad is watching over me?" Jon asked. "I hope not. That is too embarrassing."

"Mom said they put our dog Lucky to sleep. Will I die when I go to sleep too?" asked four-year-old Sam.

Tammy heard Mom say, "Sweets can kill you." She thought Aunt Margaret died from eating too much candy.

Five-year-old Ned wondered, "Grandma said God loved Grandpa so much he took him to heaven. Doesn't God love me that much?"

"Grandpa went to heaven," Alice thought. "Why can't I go too?"

The nature of the grieving child

Grieving children need to feel that they are being heard and understood. Many sensitive issues will arise, and feelings of worry, sadness, rage, terror, shame, abandonment, and guilt may emerge. *Children Also Grieve* helps adults to create a safe environment that meets the needs of all grieving children, giving them the freedom and security to express thoughts and feelings, and to feel that they are listened to in the process.

Six-year-old Nancy expressed great anger at Mrs. Lee, her teacher, for her lack of acknowledgement of Nancy's father's death. After the first week of school she bravely told Mrs. Lee that her father had died of cancer. Mrs. Lee never responded to her, and Nancy waited and waited for a reply.

Every child is unique and so is the way he or she grieves. A helpful attitude is one that allows the child to be the expert: "Teach me about your grief and I will be with you." So often, we as adults try to prescribe to children how they should think and feel, instead of allowing them to tell us where they are in their grieving process.

How to help children express grief

Share the experience of looking at family pictures in order to open a dialogue and allow the expression of memories.

Allow children to tell their story over and over again. Using tools such as writing, role-playing, and re-enactment, boys and girls can safely project feelings and thoughts about their loss, and may feel some relief from expressing their inward thoughts outwardly.

Provide reality checks such as allowing the child to call their surviving parent during the school day or visit the school nurse. These interventions reassure girls and boys that they and their family are ok. Grieving children are often preoccupied with their own health and the health of their loved ones.

Encourage memory projects where the child creates physical objects in order to remember his or her feelings and share them. A memory book is a collection of feelings and thoughts conveyed through artwork, poetry, and story-telling that allows the child to re-experience memories in a safe way. It serves as a useful tool to enable children to talk about the person who has died and to open discussion.

Suggest letter writing as another tool that allows children to express unrecognized feelings.

Recommend drawing as a means of expressing unacknowledged feelings. Children can create pictures of how they visualized their loved one dying, of the hospital or funeral scene, or their image of where their loved one is now.

Promote support groups for children and families as a way to share memories and not feel alone throughout the grief process.

Create rituals that allow children and their families to express their grief. Making Grandmother's favorite recipe, visiting Uncle Joe's grave together, or singing Aunt Betsy's favorite song helps girls and boys share their memories with others.

Become a grief team by including the child as a recognized mourner. Adults can model memories and share the child's grief, allowing children to safely express their thoughts and feelings.

Conclusion

Many young people will experience grief and trauma throughout their childhood. They need caring adults to create an oasis of safety to explore these sensitive experiences. School violence, war, terrorism, and global unrest may act as traumatic triggers for many of the pre-existing grief issues of our children. These pre-existing grief issues may have arisen from sudden fatal accidents and deaths due to illness, suicide, and homicide.

There are also many non-death related issues that have a similar effect on children. Loss of family stability owing to separation and divorce, violence and abuse, unemployment, bullying and victimization, foster care, multiple relocation, parental imprisonment, sexuality and gender issues, military deployment and service, and family alcohol and drug addiction are a few of the many grief issues that may affect a child.

Grief feelings and thoughts are continuous and ever-changing, inundating children's lives like waves on the ocean. Thoughts and feelings may arrive without warning, and children may feel unable to cope with their enormity in a home or school setting. When children can express previously hidden emotions, they gain a greater under-standing of themselves and allow the adults around them a deeper insight into their grief process.

"What we can mention, we can manage." If we, as caring and educated adults, are incapable of discussing important, and to some degree universal, life issues, how then are children to learn how to discuss them? Who will model such thoughts for them? If professionals and parents provide grief vocabulary, resources, and educational inter-ventions, they can create a safe haven for expressing these profound and difficult life issues.

Children Also Grieve can become a bridge of communica-tion between the world of fear, isolation, and the loneliness of grief to the world of truth, compassion, and dignity for the grieving child. This book enables children and the caring adults around them to recognize the pre-ciousness of life, the endurance of love, and the importance of thoughtful listening.

Bibliography

Resources for children

A Terrible Thing Happened: A Story for Children Who Have Witnessed Violence or Trauma by M. Holmes. (2000) Washington, DC: Magination Press.
Sherman explains something terrible has happened to him and learns to talk about it. (Ages 5–9)

After a Murder: A Workbook for Grieving Kids by The Dougy Center. (2001) Portland, OR: The Dougy Center.
This is a useful workbook for children who have experienced a murder. (Ages 8–12)

Bart Speaks Out: Breaking the Silence on Suicide by L. Goldman. (1998) Los Angeles, CA: Western Psychological Services.
This is an excellent, user-friendly, interactive storybook for children on the sensitive topic of suicide. (Ages 4–9)

Be a Friend: Children Who Live with HIV Speak by A. Best, P.A. Pizzo and L.S. Wiener (1994) Morton Grove, IL: Albert Whitman & Co.
This is a wonderful book written by children with AIDS and those who work with them. (Ages 5–11)

Everything Changes, But Love Endures: Explaining Hospice to Children by K. Carney. (1999) Wethersfield, CT: Dragonfly Publishing.
This is a helpful resource for young children that provides age-appropriate explanations about hospices. (Ages 4–9)

Resources for adults

Breaking the Silence: A Guide to Help Children with Complicated Grief/Suicide, Homicide, AIDS, Violence, and Abuse, Second Edition by L. Goldman. (2001) New York, NY: Taylor and Francis.
This is a clearly written guide for adults to help children and teens with complex grief issues. It includes specific chapters on suicide, homicide, AIDS, violence and abuse, guidelines for educators, national resources, and an annotated bibliography.

Life and Loss: A Guide to Help Grieving Children, Second Edition by L. Goldman. (2000) New York, NY: Taylor and Francis.
This is a practical and comprehensive resource for caring adults working with children's issues of grief and loss. It provides information, resources, hands-on activities, a model of a goodbye visit for children, and an annotated bibliography.

Lost for Words: Loss and Bereavement Awareness Training by J. Holland, R. Dance, N. MacManus and C. Stitt. (2005) London: Jessica Kingsley Publishers.
Lost for Words is an innovative "loss awareness" training package designed for teachers and caregivers supporting children who are experiencing bereavement, be it through death or any other kind of loss.

Raising Our Children to Be Resilient: A Guide to Helping Children Cope with Trauma in Today's World by L. Goldman. (2005) New York, NY: Taylor and Francis.
This is a complete resource on traumatic grief in today's world, including children's voices on events such as war, terrorism, school violence, and bullying, with age-appropriate resources and interventions. It highlights family, school, and community resources that empower children to enhance their natural resilience.

Without You: Children and Young People Growing Up with Loss and its Effects by T. Granot. (2005) London: Jessica Kingsley Publishers.
This book provides practical and sensitive advice on supporting grieving children. Granot explores the consequences grief can have on children's development, and discusses unresolved loss for adults.

About Linda Goldman

Linda Goldman is a Fellow in Thanatology: Death, Dying, and Bereavement (FT) with degrees in counseling and early childhood education. She is a Licensed Clinical Professional Counselor and a National Certified Counselor.

Linda has a private grief therapy practice in Chevy Chase, Maryland, working with children, teenagers, families with prenatal loss, and grieving adults. She presents workshops and courses on children and grief and teaches as an adjunct professor on the Graduate Counseling Program at Johns Hopkins University.

Linda has worked as a consultant for Head Start, the national program helping to address the needs of disadvantaged children and their families, and currently serves on a number of advisory boards: SPEAK (Suicide Prevention Education Awareness for Kids), RAINBOWS for Our Children, and TAPS (The Tragedy Assistance Program for Survivors) of a military death. She is a past board member of ADEC (Association for Death Education and Counseling).

In 1998, *The Washingtonian Magazine* named her as one of the top therapists in the Maryland, Virginia, and District of Columbia area and, in 2001, the same publication recommended Linda to people in need of therapy after the 9/11 terrorist attacks in New York. She was actively involved in organized responses to the trauma that followed the attacks, conducting workshops and writing a number of articles. In 2003, Linda received the ADEC Clinical Practice Award.

Linda Goldman is the author of *Life and Loss, Breaking the Silence, Raising Our Children to Be Resilient*, and *Bart Speaks Out*.

Linda lives with her husband Michael, son Jonathan and their two wonderful Tibetan Terriers, Henry and Tashi, in Chevy Chase, Maryland.